To: Ed Sterner

www.**FISHING WITH STEVE**.Net/

Go Fish!

Stephen M. Goosley

Thanks
Steve

AuthorHouse™
1663 Liberty Drive
Bloomington, IN 47403
www.authorhouse.com
Phone: 1-800-839-8640

© 2010 Stephen M. Goosley. All rights reserved.

No part of this book may be reproduced, stored in a retrieval system, or transmitted by any means without the written permission of the author.

First published by AuthorHouse   7/23/2010

ISBN: 978-1-4520-3342-6 (sc)

Library of Congress Control Number: 2010907763

Printed in the United States of America
Bloomington, Indiana

This book is printed on acid-free paper.

INTRODUCTION

    In the spring of 2000 I applied for a job as assistant fishing instructor. The following summer I was the fishing instructor and was able to improve a good fishing course and make it a great fishing course.

    Every summer I teach seven separate fishing classes at a local college. I teach classes of about twenty students per class. The students range from 3rd grade up to the 9th grade. Day one is teaching basic fishing skills safety, and we have casting contest. The other three days we go out and fish at different locations. I take a group of photos of the students when they catch fish and give them their pictures on the last day of class, along with a nice certificate of the students who won or placed in the casting contest. There is a fishing class for girls only and an advanced fishing class. The students fishing skills improve by the last day of class, which makes me proud of them.

    I was lucky growing up to have my Uncle Mike who introduced me to freshwater fishing and my Uncle Bill who took me fishing in the ocean and the bay.

    Since then fishing has been a life long hobby that has brought me much joy and a part time job. It has also enabled me to share my fishing experience, which to me is an added blessing. When I take a picture of a student who has caught their first fish it is such a thrill.

    I served in the U.S. Marines for 21 years and traveled all over the U.S. and the world. My travels gave me the opportunity to fish from the shores of New Jersey, North Carolina, and California. I have fished the Colorado River area of Yuma, Arizona the Chesapeake Bay, and Lake Ferguson in Arizona. I have spear fished in Hawaii and the Philippines. I have ocean fished on numerous occasions, unfortunately I get seasick. I love the water and have scuba dived off the coast California and snorkeled the ocean in Okinawa., Japan.

    Fishing with Steve was written to encourage others to share the joys of fishing with the younger generation. Our great Nation is rich with rivers, lakes, ponds and creeks and our children should all enjoy the great outdoors.

ACKNOWLEDGEMENTS

I would like to thank Gail from Horizons for Youth who hired me and her staff, Carrie Holly and Jane. The print shop at Northampton Community College who takes care of my printing needs and the Pennsylvania Fish and Game Commission, who have provided me with great information about fishing. The publisher of Angler and Boater for their excellent magazine which I use to find places to fish and helps me with my teaching.

Bob my bus driver who takes us safely to our fishing spots. My past fishing assistants and my current fishing assistant Eddy and his wife Linda who makes the fishing casting contest certificates. The student helpers who help the younger students learn to bait, apply tackle and cast. And a special thanks to Frank Whelan who has been a writer for over 30 years. Frank transformed my rough draft into a good readable story.

Steve caught this 17 inch bass at Raystown Lake)

Chapter One

When the sunlight came shining through his window that Saturday morning Darien was more excited than he had been since Christmas. Finally he was going to meet Steve "The Fishing Guy"!

Darien's mother had promised him if he was good in school and made good grades she would sign him up for a fishing class with Steve. All Darien's friends had told him what a "cool" guy Steve was. A fishing instructor at the local community college, every summer Steve taught basic fishing to students from third grade to ninth grade.

The day before the class Darien and his father went to the store and bought a fishing pole, a tackle box, hooks, bobbers, and weights. They took the fishing rod out of the package and put it together. After attaching the reel to the pole they threaded the string thru the eyelets, careful not to miss any or to wrap the string around the pole.

Next Darien and his father tied a plastic sinker to his fishing line so he could practice his casting out in the yard. He had heard from some of his friends that Steve had a casting contest on the first day of class. Darien wanted to do well at casting. He had heard prizes were offered for the best cast and he hoped to be lucky enough to win one.

His Dad carefully showed Darien how to cast. Now the boy wanted to try. He took the fishing rod and raised it over his head. Then he flung the pole forward pressing the button that released the fishing line. It went high and to the right and into the tree in the yard. "Now I'll never win a prize," Darien said disappointedly. But his Dad told him not to worry. "If you practice you will get better" he said, "Steve will teach you how to make an accurate cast."

The first day of the fishing class was held in a classroom at the college where Steve worked. It started at nine and ended at noon.

Early that morning Darien put his fishing pole and tackle box in the car and made sure his Mom had the medical release form. During the twenty minute ride to the college the boy was so excited that he could barely sit still. When they got there Darien jumped from the car, took his fishing rod from the trunk and headed for the big classroom building.

At first walking, almost running, Darien entered and bounced up the stairs ahead of his Mom then he suddenly stopped, turned and saw the number on the door that they had been told was Steve's classroom.

In front of the room was a middle aged man with a stocky built and a nice smile. "Hello," the man said to Darien "my name is Steve You must be Darien."

Darien had never seen anybody dressed quite like Steve before. He wore a really "cool" white canvas fishing hat and a fishing vest which had his fishing license attached and a pair of fingernail clippers.

Darien was fascinated by the pockets of Steve's vest. They were bulging with fishing tackle. His belt had pouches on it with needle nose pliers and regular pliers tucked into them.

Steve told Darien to put his pole by the wall and have a seat. Then the fishing instructor gave his Mom a colorful folder filled with pamphlets. Steve explained that they were all about fish and fishing in Pennsylvania and that her son would need to study them as part of the course. Darien said goodbye to his Mom who promised to pick him up at noon.

Gradually more students arrived until eleven seats were filled. Steve gave their parents the same kind of folder that he had given Darien's Mom.

Chapter Two

Steve welcomed all the students to the fishing class.

"Boys and girls" he said pointing to three people next to him "this is my assistant Eddy and my helpers Alex and Ashley. They are going to make the course fun and see that you learn to fish safely."

Steve then asked everyone to introduce themselves and tell where they went to school. Some came from cities like Allentown and Bethlehem. Others lived in other parts of the Lehigh Valley like Emmaus and Schnecksville.

There were two girls in the class. Darien was surprised. He did not know that girls liked to fish.

Half the students in class had been fishing before and the other half never had.

"You are all lucky to live here in Pennsylvania," Steve told the class. "It has some of the best fishing spots of the whole world." Darien was surprised to learn that his home state had more than 83,000 miles of streams and rivers over 4000 lakes and 160 different kinds of fish.

"My goal," said Steve "is to teach every one of you how to tie a fishing knot, bait a hook and attach bobbers and weights. By the last day of class you will also learn how to hook fish, and release them safely back into the water." Steve promised the class that everyone would catch at least one fish before the end of the course.

Darien could hardly wait. Steve told the class before they could catch fish they had to learn how to do it safely. Fishing hooks were sharp, he warned. Removing them would require a trip to the hospital. Darien listened as Steve talked of how important it was to make sure no one was to close to you when you were casting. Look before you cast, Steve said and do not try to fish the same spot.

"Most hook accidents come from carelessness," Steve told the class. "When you move from one spot to another, attach your hook to an eyelet on the pole and carry the pole straight up."

"Accidents," he added "happen when you're not careful when untangling your line or your attaching bait to the line and somebody accidentally walks by and catches your pole with their foot. This yanks the line and pulls the hook into your finger! Use a finger nail clipper to cut your fishing line not a knife."

"Another safety rule," said Steve, "is do not try to catch a snake or other animals. They are wild animals not pets."

Steve gave an example of what could happen from his days in the Marine Corps. A fellow Marine, stationed with him in the desert, foolishly tried to catch a rattlesnake with his bare hands. The poisonous snake bit him and his finger started to turn black. Fortunately he was rushed to the hospital so he would not lose his finger. "This Marine was a fighter pilot," Steve noted, "if he had lost his finger his career as a flyer would have been over."

"Clothing is also very important," Steve said. "A hat is protection from the sun, wear sneakers or boots not sandals to protect your feet, use sun screen, drink plenty of water, do not go in the water, do not wander off alone, respect each other, and listen to your instructors.

Steve told the class about a helper who wore sandals when fishing the Lehigh River. "He broke two rules," Steve said, "he went into the water and he wore sandals."

When the helper went into the water to try to free his line from being stuck, his sandal came off and was sweep away by the current. "It floated down the river never to be seen again" Steve said. "He had to fish the rest of the day with one sandal."

His safety lecture finished, Steve told the class it was time to take a break.

Darien took the time to get to know his classmates Anthony, Delila, and Destiny. They were cousins and were just as excited as he was about going fishing for the first time.

When the break was over the class learned about rigging poles, casting, and hooking fish.

Steve had Eddy demonstrate how to tie a clinch knot which is used to securely attach a swivel to the fishing line. Eddy threaded the line through the swivel made a loop and wrapped the lower section of line around the upper section six times. went through the lower loop and back up through the new loop. Next he pulled the line tight and the swivel was securely attached.

To finish the knot Eddy trimmed the excess line off the knot with his finger nail clippers. Steve then showed how easy it was to add and remove hooks, lures, jigheads, spoons, leaders, and crankbaits using the snap swivel. For Darien all these words were new and he paid close attention to Steve.

Helper Ashley showed how to attach weight to the fishing line about six inches above the swivel.

The weights Steve used were a little unleaded ball with wings on them so you could add and remove the weight easily with a pair of pliers. The weights would give more distance while casting and take the hook deeper into the water. "Don't try to use your teeth to cut the line" Steve warned the class. "Not only are there germs but you could also break your teeth."

Steve's other helper Alex showed how to attach a bobber to the line which looked easy to do. The bobber was attached about six inches above the swivel

The bobber had a spring loaded button on it which helped make it easy to attach to the line. It made it easy for the fisherman to hook the fish and it kept the hook off the bottom so it would not get stuck in the rocks or stuck in the weeds.

Steve told the class they must lift the tip of the pole when they saw the bobber go under the water. "If you jerk too hard on the pole," he said, "you will pull the hook out of the fish's mouth."

Now the class was ready to begin rigging their poles. They practiced tying the clinch knot, and attached a swivel, bobber, and size eight hooks to the fishing line. Steve, Eddy, Alex and Ashley, helped Darien and the others.

Once the poles were rigged, Steve had the class remove the hooks and get ready for the casting contest. This was the moment Darien had been waiting for all morning.

Chapter Three

The class lined up and carried their poles in the safe position as they walked outside to the grassy area. Eddy carried three hoola hoops. Alex and Ashley carried the tackle boxes.

Steve had the class face him. They were standing ten foot apart for safety. "Ok" he said, "the most important thing is to look before you cast your line."

Steve had Eddy set the three hoola hoops about twenty-five feet away from the line Then he had them separated a good distance from each other.

Steve then demonstrated the three different ways to cast.

Overhand was the first. He told the class to think of a clock. The top of your head was twelve o' clock. Next he said you take the tip of the pole back to about two o'clock and come forward and release the line at about eleven o'clock.

Steve cast the line with the weight and bobber on it. The bobber went right to the center of the hoola hoop

Next Steve showed the side arm and backhand cast. 'The backhand cast is used when standing under trees," Steve explained.

It was now the classes turn to cast. Fishing lines were all over the place and not even near the target hoola hoops. The fishing instructors started to help the students correct their casting mistakes and everyone was making improvements.

It was now time for the casting contest and the three winners would get certificates for first, second, and third place. The class was divided into three groups of four and placed single file in front of the hoola hoops.

The first person in each line was ten feet in front of the other three students for safety. Steve and a helper were behind the hoola hoops, which were twenty five feet away from the class. Eddy and the other helper were with Darien and the other students just in case they needed help.

"Casting the line with the weight and bobber on it and putting the bobber into the center of the hoola hoop is your goal," Steve said.

The students were given three attempts to score a bull's eye or to get as close as they could. Steve and the helpers would mark the spot that the bobber landed. The best three marks would be the winners.

Darien was the second to the last student to go. None of the other students had put the bobber in the center of the hoola hoops.

The boy was nervous. This was his last cast and he was not close enough to place in the top three.

Steve sensed his fear.

"Relax and concentrate, Darien," he said, "and you will do well."

With these words of encouragement in his ear Darien cast his line. The bobber landed right on the outside of the hoola hoop. He was now in first place.

There was only one other student, the girl Destiny had not cast. Her first attempt was short and to the right. Her second cast went over the top of the hoola hoop by about five feet.

As he had with Darien Steve told Destiny to relax and concentrate. The young girl brought the tip of the pole back and with a look of determination cast the line with the bobber at the hoola hoop. It landed right in the center of the hoop. Destiny took first place.

Everyone, even Darien was cheering. He was happy with second place and the big improvement in his casting.

Steve had the class line up for a picture. He promised them they would receive a copy of the picture on the last day of class. Then the winners had their pictures taken for their certificates in a casting pose with their fishing poles.

Steve congratulated everyone on the good job they did. He wrote Destiny's name on the board for first place, Darien's for second place, and Anthony's for third place. Then they leaned their poles up against the wall and returned to their seats. "Ok class," Steve said. "Now its story time."

Chapter Four

"All good fishermen," Steve said, "have tall and small fish tales to tell."

Steve went first as Darien and the class listened intently

"I was fishing with a group of my students on the Delaware River," Steve began.

"One of them, Peter, had his fishing pole baited for catfish and it was resting on top of a stick with a Y shape poked into the ground. He was proud of his new fishing pole that his mother had just bought him."

"Getting thirsty, Peter walked up the hill to get a drink from the ice chest. Just as he put his hand around a can of soda he heard a loud bang. A big catfish had snatched his bait and had pulled the fishing pole into the water. He reached the river bank just in time to see his pole disappear under the water".

"Peter was worried about what his mother was going to say about him losing his pole. I gave him another fishing pole to use for the rest of the day."

"A while later Gabriel cast his line out into the water. Gabe had a bite and he set the hook and started to reel the line in. It was a struggle. His pole was almost bent in half.

It was then he saw it was not a fish, but Peter's fishing pole he had caught.

Ashley, thinking quickly, grabbed Peter's pole as it started to bend and shake. She saw the catfish was still on the hook. Skillfully reeling it in she was surprised. The catfish was a big one!

Peter was overjoyed about getting his fishing pole back with the catfish on it. So boys and girls this story had a happy ending. But it also teaches a valuable lesson never leave your fishing gear unguarded."

Delilah was next. "I went fishing with my dad last summer at a lake. We were in a boat and not getting even a nibble. I was bored with fishing and laid my pole down and put my hand in the water.

I was moving it back and forth when suddenly something bit my finger. I yanked my finger out of the water and screamed. Then I saw a small sunfish was flopping around inside the boat, I had caught a sunfish with my finger. My father could not believe it."

Anthony came next. "My father was fishing at Lake Nockamixon and caught a great white shark." Some students said "Wow" but others laughed. Steve, Eddy, and the helpers Alex, and Ashley were among those laughing.

"Good fish story" said Steve. "That is definitely a tall fish tale. Sharks cannot live in freshwater so Anthony's father must have caught the Great White Shark in the ocean. I don't want you students to be afraid of swimming in lakes or fresh water."

But Anthony had a big smile on his face. He was proud of his fish tale because he had made everyone laugh or gasp. Darien looked forward to the time when he had a fish tale to tell.

It was almost time for the parents to pick up the students. "Before you go I want to give you some important information about going fishing tomorrow," Steve said."

We are going to Moyer's Lake. They have a trout pond but you have to pay to catch fish out of the pond. The cost is two dollars and fifty cents and you have to have permission from your parents to bring fish home to eat. There were other ponds there to fish for free with plenty of bass, sunfish, and catfish."

Then, Steve announced the class had a homework assignment! Darien and the other students were shocked. Wasn't it summer time? Wasn't fishing supposed to be fun?

." Calm down," Steve said. "In order to become good fishermen you have to have knowledge. You're assignment for this evening is fish identification. I want every student to pick a different fish to write about. And draw if you draw it you will get extra credit!"

Just as Steve finished Darien saw his Dad's car and those of the other parents pulling into the parking lot. He could not wait to tell him what he had learned and what fun he had.

Chapter Five

From the big smile on his face Darien's Dad could tell his son had enjoyed himself He told his dad they we're were going to Moyers Lake the next day to fish . He asked permission to bring a trout home to eat. "That would be fine, but only one," his Dad said.

Then Darien told his Dad that he had won second place in the fishing contest.

"I am proud of you son," he said.

Darien's Dad laughed when he said he had a homework assignment.

"What do you have to do," he asked?

"I have to write about a brook trout and draw a picture of one."

"That's a good idea. It will help you learn about trout and give you practice in reading and writing. You like to draw, so that part will be easy for you".

"Darien, you seem uneasy, what else on your mind," he asked

"I needed a fishing hat to protect me from the sun's rays and I would like a fishing vest to carry my tackle in."

"Is that all," his father asked.

"I still want to ask you something."

"What else?"

"I also need a pair of needle nose pliers with a holder to fit on my belt and finger nail clippers with a nylon cord attached to hang on my vest."

"What for," he said."

"The pliers are for removing hooks from the fish and attaching weights to the fishing line and the finger nail clippers are for cutting the fishing line."

"Well you did a good job in school this past year, and you have been doing your chores around the house, and you do keep your room clean and neat. You have earned your wish; we can go to the store now."

"Yippee" Darien shouted.

Once they got home from the store, Darien put his fishing stuff in the garage. Then he ran to his room with the bag with the vest, hat, pliers, and finger nail clippers. He put on the hat and vest and looked liked a miniature version of Steve the fishing guy. He showed his mom and dad. "Now you look like a real fisherman," they said.

Then Darien asked his Father if he had any empty film containers.

'What do you need them for?"

"Steve puts his swivels and weights in them and they fit perfect in the vest pockets."

"Good idea" said Dad, and then gave Darien some empty photo canisters.

Darien transferred all his fishing tackle from the tackle box into the vest. The only thing he would have to carry now was my pole and bait.

When he finished dinner it was time for Darien to do my fishing homework. His Mom gave him the folder with the fishing literature in it. The front of the folder had a catchy phrase on it, "Catch Me If You Can" and a picture of a fish. Inside there was a lot of information about fishing in the state of Pennsylvania.

It included Pennsylvania's Fishing Laws and Regulations, Fishing Getting Started Pennsylvania's State fishing Records, Pamphlets, Angler Award Program, What's Your Fish I.Q., Where to Fish Map, Fish Identification Guide, Fish Parts Word Search, Pennsylvania's Fish Facts Game, Fish Art Contest, Photo contest, How Fish Hear, See and Smell, Water Pollution and more. Steve got all this information free from Pennsylvania's Fish and Game Commission. He had also suggested they might even go on the commission's website. .

Darien's homework was to write about and draw the Brook Trout, Pennsylvania's State Fish. He learned from the information in the folder that the state fishing record from 2004 was a Brook Trout that was over twenty-one inches long and weighed over four pounds.

Darien also learned, from Popular Sportfish of Pennsylvania where the Brook Trout live, how to catch them, and when to fish for them. The Trout identification sheet gives him a good colored picture of the brook trout to draw the fish.

On the same sheet were five other trout the Brown, Rainbow, Golden Rainbow, Steelhead, and Lake Trout. "I would love to catch a Golden Rainbow Trout," Darien thought to himself.

"Steve said that he learns a lot about fishing from reading about fishing. I am going to read about fishing so I can become a good fisherman just like Steve. I am going to ask my dad to subscribe to Angler and Boater Magazine which has a special section in it for kids."

Darien worked hard that drawing and writing his assignment on the Brook Trout. When he was done Darien showed them to his dad and mom.

"You will get an "A+," his mom said.

Tired after a long day Darien got ready for bed. Soon he was dreaming of the fish he would catch.

Chapter Six

The next morning Darien's Dad drove him to fishing class.

"Now remember," his Dad said as they drove into the parking lot. "We agreed that you could bring home only one trout to eat."

"I agree," Darien said nodding his head.

They drove up to a big yellow school bus. Steve, Eddy, Ashley, and Alex were all there helping to load the bus for the trip to Moyers Lake.

Steve greeted them.

"Are you ready to catch some fish Darien," he said.

"Yes Sir," the boy replied.

"Nice hat and vest," Steve said.

When he heard those words Darien could not have grinned any wider.

Steve collected the boy's home work and told Darien to give Eddy his fishing pole.

Then Darien found a seat on the bus next to his friend Anthony. Both boys were excited and began talking about all the fish they were going to catch.

The bus was quickly loaded with fishing nets, an ice chest, a water cooler, tackle boxes and extra fishing poles. Steve thanked everyone for turning in and doing there homework and said he would grade them and give them back Thursday the last day of class.

Steve introduced the class to the bus driver. His name was Bob and he was wearing a fishing vest too.

"Wow" said Anthony, "Way cool."

Bob said hello to us and reminded us that we needed to follow the safety rules for riding on the school bus. "That means no standing up while the bus is moving," he said.

"Did everybody like the information I gave you about fishing," Steve asked.

"Yes," the class shouted back with one voice.

"Ok class now I want to tell you about Moyers Lake," he began. "It is between Coopersburg and Limeport in a wooded area. There is a ten acre lake and two trout ponds. To fish the trout ponds you have to pay $2.75 for the trout you catch. But the big lake was free and had a lot of Bass, Sunfish, and Catfish in it."

"You have to be careful though," Steve warned "There are geese, ducks, and two swans at the lake. If you come to close you could accidentally hook them. "Also," he added "the lake has bathroom facilities, a snack shop, and bait and tackle shop, and a lunch and game room."

Steve asked the class a few questions about their assignment and was pleased with their answers. "I see you've done your homework," he said. "Now let's go fishing."

The trip to Moyers Lake took about twenty- five minutes of traveling time. The place was beautiful and the class was really excited.

"Now before we get off the bus," Steve said. "I want you to remember most importantly that you obey the fishing rules. But before we start fishing we are going to take a tour around the lake."

Darien, Anthony and the rest of the class piled off the bus. They helped unload the equipment and then began the tour. As they walked Steve showed them where everything was including the bathrooms.

When the tour was over a Steve introduced them to Gail.

"Good morning boys and girls," she said with a big smile on her face, "My name is Gail. I am in charge here at Moyers Lake. We hope you all have a great day of fishing and will help you if you need anything."

Steve bought some bait for the class to fish with. He bought mealy worms, night crawlers, and two dozen minnows which were good for catching bass. Each student got two minnows. The class was then divided into four groups of three students per instructor.

Darien was in Steve's group. It was decided they would fish the cement pond for trout. Steve helped his group rig their poles with a number eight hook on the swivel. Then he attached a weight and bobber to the fishing line.

Destiny and Delilah were in Steve's group with Darien. He showed the three of them how to attach a mealy worm to the hook. They squirmed as Steve threaded them on the hook. "I expect you to know how to put your own bait on the hook by the last day of fishing class," Steve said. Then they went down to the cement trout pond.

Looking into the pond the students noticed a bunch of Rainbow Trout and one Golden Rainbow Trout. All were bigger than ten inches long.

Darien knew with one look he wanted to catch the gold one which was about sixteen inches long. "You will have to be pretty lucky to catch that one," Steve told Darien, when he saw the boy had his eye on the big shiny fish. "No one in my class has ever caught a Golden Rainbow trout."

The three students put their rods in the water and watched as the fish attacked the bait. Destiny had a bite. But she was so excited she pulled the bait right out of the trout's mouth before he took it.

Delilah had a bite and set the hook with Steve coaching her. She had a seventeen inch Rainbow Trout on the line and it was giving her a good fight. Steve told Delilah to keep the tip of the pole down, reel it in slowly, and enjoy the fight.

Finally the trout was next to the wall. "Ok, Delilah," Steve instructed her, "lift the trout slowly out of the water." The fish was wiggling and shaking the whole way along the wall. The girl's fishing pole was bent now and as soon as the fish cleared the wall Delilah moved the pole towards land with the fish shaking violently.

Steve grabbed the trout and showed us how to removed the hook and put the fish on a stringer. Steve had Delilah hold the trout by the stringer and took a picture of her with the big rainbow trout. Then he put the trout in a little pond next to the cement pond to keep the fish alive until they were ready to clean him.

Destiny, hooked the next fish. It was another big rainbow trout. This time she took her time reeling it in. Soon Steve was taking her picture with her prize catch.

Darien told himself he was glad Delilah and Destiny did not catch the golden trout. He wanted to catch that one.

Destiny and Delilah joined the other students at the big pond. But Darien kept pulling his bait out of the water when the rainbow trout came near it and casting it back at the golden rainbow trout, which was the only fish he wanted to catch.

But the golden rainbow trout did not offer a nibble at Darien's bait. 'Maybe he is just not hungry," the boy thought.

Steve saw that Darien was getting disappointed. "Why don't we change the bait from a mealy worm to a night crawler," Steve said. He handed the boy a night crawler. Without thinking about it he threaded the worm on the hook! "Wow, I did it," said the excited Darien.

Carefully aiming the bait Darien dropped it into the pond as close as he could get it to the golden trout. Without warning Darien felt a sharp hard tug. The golden trout had taken his bait.

Steve could not believe it. "Relax Darien and reel him in slowly," he said to the boy. "If you don't, you could lose him."

Darien was so excited it was hard for him to concentrate on what he was supposed to be doing. The other students heard the excitement and came over to the pond. They were cheering the boy on.

Darien slowly and carefully reeled the golden trout near the wall. He remembered that Steve had told him that most of his students lost their trout by jerking the fish out of the water and causing them to shake off the hook.

At last the golden trout was pulled out of the water. He was shaking wildly all the way up the length of the wall. Although his pole was bent practically in half; Darien stayed focused on what he was doing.

Steve was standing, waiting for the fish towards the land and him. The golden trout was above the land but it flopped off the hook. Soon it was flopping up and down trying to bounce back into the water.

But Darien was not about to let that happen. He blocked the fish from going back into the water. Steve grabbed the golden trout and put him on the stringer.

By now everybody was cheering. Gail the lake's owner was there with big smile on her face and a camera in her hand. She said she was going to put the fish and Darien on her web site!

Darien could not believe his luck. He had caught his first fish and it was a whopper. He would not have to tell tall tales at fish story time because now he had a real one to tell.

Chapter Seven

Darien was so happy and could not wait to get home to show his Mom and Dad his catch.

But for now he went over to a small dock to fish with Eddy, Steve's assistant.

"Come on, Darien," said Eddy. "I am going to show you how to attach a live minnow to your hook. Then were going to fish for bass."

Eddy showed the boy how to hook the minnow in the upper mouth, middle of the back, or tail.

"Now be careful, Darien," Eddy said. "Cast the line gently so you don't jerk the minnow off the hook"

Darien did as Eddy had told him. He could see the bobber moving as the minnow swam. Suddenly there was a tug on the line. But before Darien could react the bass took the minnow right off the hook.

The boy reeled in the line and put another minnow on the hook by himself. Soon he was ready to cast again. The minnow was in the water swimming sudden when the bass struck again.

But this time Darien was ready. He set the hook into the bass's mouth. But big fish was no pushover. It jumped out of the water, full of fight.

Eddy told the boy to let the bass fight and tire himself out and then reel him in steadily. Darien had developed a steady hand. Soon the bass was next to the dock. Eddy had the fish net ready.

The bass was on the dock now flopping and still fighting to get off the hook. Eddy grabbed the fish by its lower lip with his thumb and index finger. He held it up and removed the hook.

Steve told Darien to grab the bass so he could take a picture. The boy was nervous, but wanted a picture to show his parents. Darien gripped the bass with his thumb and index finger as hard as he could and faced the camera with his bass held high and a big smile.

Steve took the picture. "Ok, Darien, now tell me," Steve asked. "What kind of bass did you catch?"

Darien was not prepared to answer. Steve quickly saw the puzzled look on his face.

"It's a largemouth bass," the instructor said. "You can tell that because of its greenish color and that its upper jaw extends beyond the back edge of the eye."

Steve measured Darien's catch. It was sixteen inches long. He then showed the boy how to put the bass back in the water. "He was a brave fish," said Steve. "This way he will live to fight another day."

Darien headed off the dock and joined the rest of the class who were getting ready for lunch. Everybody had caught at least one fish.

Just as they were getting ready to eat the class heard noise that sounded like it was coming from the dock. A young boy had accidentally hooked a duckling in the neck. His grandfather, who had taken the boy fishing that day, was trying to help. But the duck was in a panic and so was the boy. The duckling's Mother and brothers and sisters were quacking too and staying close to him.

Steve ran out on the dock and pulled his needle nose pliers out of his pouch. Gail, the lake's owner joined him. She grabbed the fishing pole from the child and started to reel the line in towards the dock where Steve was waiting. When the crying duckling was close to the dock Steve grabbed it gently and carried it out of the water. Gail had to use the fishing pole to keep the mother duck away.

When Steve finally had the shaking duckling in his hands he grabbed the hook with his needle nose pliers and pulled it carefully out of its neck. Then he gently put the duckling back into the water and it swam over to its mother. Steve and Gail had saved the duckling and everyone was cheering.

Chapter Eight

After lunch Steve had all his students come over to the fish cleaning table. Gail agreed to show the class how to gut and clean the fish they had caught.

Gail showed them her filet knife. She told the class it was very sharp. "That is why I have to be careful when I use it," she said.

Delilah brought her catch to the table first. Steve removed the Rainbow Trout from the stringer and handed the fish to Gail. She placed it on a special fish cleaning board. It had a spring loaded clamp on it to hold the fish by the tail.

First she cut the head off, and then she sliced opened the trout. The class had never seen the inside of a fish before. They were amazed to see its heart was still pumping even after it was cut out! "Gross," one of them said.

Then Gail rinsed the fish with water. She put it in a freezer bag with Delilah's name on it. Steve told the girl to put the trout in the ice chest to keep it fresh.

Darien's Golden Rainbow Trout was the last fish to be cleaned.

"Steve," the boy said before Gail could begin, "I don't want her to gut my fish. I want to take it home and have it mounted to hang on the wall in my room."

Steve laughed and said "Ok you can do that". Then Darien put the trout in the freezer bag and put him in the ice chest to stay fresh.

Darien went over by his friend Gabriel. He was fishing for a catfish. Gabriel was using a piece of chicken liver and it was stinky, just the way Catfish like them.

Darien, hoping to catch a sunfish, baited his pole with a night crawler but no sooner had he put it in the water when he noticed Gabriel's fishing pole bent in half. His friend had hooked a big catfish and it was giving Gabriel quite a fight.

Steve's helper Ashley came over to help Gabriel. Darien and the rest of the class were just as excited as Gabriel. Finally Gabriel had the catfish on land. It was a whopper! Gabriel posed with his catfish for a picture.

The Catfish was seventeen inches long. After he measured it Steve told the boy it was a Bullhead Catfish. Then the instructor removed the hook with his needle nose pliers and showed us how to handle a catfish.

Steve showed the class its sharp spines and fins. He told them the whiskers on a catfish were used to find food. "Never put your finger in a catfish's mouth they have sharp teeth" Steve said.

Practically everyone had caught at least one sunfish today. "Sunfish are a food source for larger game fish," Steve told the class. "The Bluegill sunfish is the most common sunfish caught today because they like ponds and warm water."

Steve had barely finished talking when Darien's bobber started to jump in the water. The boy set the hook and started to reel in his first sunfish. It was getting close to shore when out of the blue came a big bass. It took Darien's sunny right off my hook! "Wow," .said the boy, "that happened so fast." Steve's helper Alex was laughing and said that it happen to him once.

"Time to clean up and pack up" Steve yelled.

Everyone was getting their fishing gear together and heading for the bus where Bob was waiting to load us up. Steve and his helpers made sure all the students had all their fishing gear and their lunch sacks. Then he made the class pick-up all of the trash on the ground whether they had made it or not.

Then the class thanked Gail for the helping us have a good day fishing. After the class washed their hands Steve got them on the bus. He counted heads to make sure no one was missing.

"Did everybody have fun" Steve asked.

"Yes," they all shouted.

Then Steve took a fish count. The class had caught twelve trout, eighteen sunfish, six bass and one catfish. And included were two spotted frogs and a turtle.

"You were a really good class today," Steve said. "You followed the rules and you listened. I am very proud of you." Everybody smiled back at Steve.

On the bus ride home everyone was talking about the fish they caught. Darien could not wait to get back and show and tell his parents.

Chapter Nine

That night Darien's parents enjoyed hearing him tell all about his fishing adventures. The boy was really happy when they agreed to have the Golden Rainbow Trout mounted so he could hang it in his room.

Early the next morning the class was on its way to Lake Minsi. It was located north of Bangor, Pa and Steve told them it would be around a 45 minute bus ride from the college.

On the ride Steve started to tell the students about Lake Minsi. It was a man-made lake created in the early 1970s. The park itself was about one-hundred and twenty-two acres. The lake was twenty foot deep in the middle but most areas of the lake was five foot deep. Fish species at the lake include chain pickerel, largemouth bass, walleye, brook trout, white sucker, golden shiner, brown bullhead catfish, pumpkinseed sunfish, bluegill, black crappie, and yellow perch.

"Chances are good," Steve said, "You will not catch any trout or walleye because they were in the deep cold water in the middle of the lake which you could not reach fishing from shore."

Destiny asked Steve how he knew so much about Lake Minsi. "I researched and read about the lake. And today I will be quizzing you about sunfish. I hope you all did your reading homework." Steve said.

"I did my reading about sunfish last night," Darien said. He felt sure he would be ready to answer any questions Steve would ask me.

"Next stop bait shop" Steve said as the bus pulled in.

There was a restaurant with a bait shop in the back right next to the lake. The woman and man in the shop were smiling when the class walked in. Some of the students needed to buy fishing tackle and some wanted to buy their own bait.

Darien had all the tackle he needed to fish. Steve bought plenty of bait for the class, night crawlers, mealy worms, and minnows. Darien thought it was fun watching the woman net the minnows from their tank and put them into buckets.

The lake was huge with two boat ramps for fishermen to launch their boats into the water. Steve reminded the class about snakes and safety. "Every time I bring a class here they see water snakes and some students get scared," the instructor said. "They are not poisonous and if you leave them alone they will leave you alone."

After the class unloaded it was split up into three groups. Group one stayed at the peninsula by the parking lot by the bus. Group two went to the peninsula in the middle of the lake. Group three was in between group one and group two on an angled cement wall.

Darien was in group two with Anthony and his cousins, Destiny and Delilah. Steve was their group leader. Steve told them to split up on the peninsula and pick a spot.

"There is a snake by my spot," screamed Delilah.

"It's a harmless water snake," Steve said as the brownish colored eighteen inch long. snake slide under the water and disappeared from sight. "Just leave it alone."

Darien and the class put their hooks on swivels and prepared to put bait on their hooks. Steve told the boy to put a piece of night crawler on his hook. "That is what the sunfish will like," he said.

Steve cut the worms with his fingernails. Darien used a small pair of scissors. Delilah and Destiny asked Steve to help them put mealy worms on their hooks. Anthony wanted to catch a big bass so he used a minnow. In the middle of the lake the class could see men in boats fishing for walleye and trout. "One day I would like to be fishing from a boat," thought Darien.

The group cast their lines into the water. Destiny cast her line into the weeds and started to reel it in. The pole bent in half. Destiny had hooked something. She shouted for Steve to help and he came right over to assist her.

The girl had accidentally hooked a big bull frog. Steve grabbed it and removed the hook. The frog was making a croaking sound and squirming. Steve gave Destiny the frog and took a picture of her with it. Then she released it.

In the distance Darien's group could hear the other students shouting they were catching fish. Suddenly his bobber was bouncing.

"I hope it's a sunfish," said Darien to himself.

The bobber disappeared under the water. The boy could not believe a sunfish could fight this hard. Steve who was observing Darien fighting the fish said "That's not a sunfish it's a chain pickerel."

The fish was long and skinny; it must have been sixteen inches long. Darien had the fish out of the water and on the shore. Steve told him the chain pickerel was part of the pike family of fish and could grow to more than thirty inches long. The dark chain like markings gives the fish its name. After Steve took a picture of Darien with his catch he released the fish back into the water.

Anthony, Delilah, and Destiny had caught sunfish. Darien had a bunch of bites but I just could not hook a sunfish. But by now the day was almost done.

After the class was on the bus Steve took the fish count.

"We caught one chain pickerel, twenty-five sunfish, and five bass," he told them. Steve told us we did good catching fish and everyone was baiting their own hook and releasing their own fish back into the water.

"I am proud of you," the instructor said. "Tomorrow we will be fishing at Lake Nockamixon. Maybe then Darien you will catch that sunfish."

Chapter Ten

That night Darien read the information he had gotten from Steve about sunfish. Then he went on the Pennsylvania Fish and Boat Commission web site and looked up information about Lake Nockamixon. There he learned Lake Nockamixon, was in a 5,283-acre state park. The lake is 1450 acres and is home to a variety of fish including largemouth bass, pickerel, muskies, walleyes, channel catfish, and stripers. There are also smallmouth bass, and plenty of sunfish in the lake.

Sunfish like warm water with rocky bottoms and weeds. Worms cut in small pieces and mealy worms are the best bait. Steve recommended using a size number eight hook or smaller to catch sunfish. The best time to catch sunfish is early morning or dusk. Steve says you can catch sunfish all day long and depending were you go you can catch large numbers of sunfish.

Steve took the class to a country store bait shop on route 611 called Mueller's. The women who worked there were very helpful. They had baby eels in a tank which fishermen use as bait, Brandon and his cousin Brendan accidentally, or so they said, let one of the eels out of the tank and onto the floor.

The eel slithered under the soda cases. Half of Steve's students were trying to catch the eel. It was a funny sight to see and finally the eel was caught and put back into the tank.

The class bought their bait and tackle and 15 minutes later they were at Lake Nockamixon. Crossing the bridge the class could see the lake and the area they were going to fish. Darien could not believe how huge it was.

The bus parked and the students began to unload the bus. The area they were in had a restroom, picnic tables, and a large grassy clear area to safely fish from. There were two elderly people sitting at the picnic table with fishing gear that were waiting for Steve. He introduced us to Angelo and his wife Rina. 'They are here to help you fish," he said. 'There were four helpers now and to that adds up to more fishing time."

It did not take long for everyone to have their poles rigged and baited and lines in the water fishing. Gabriel caught the first sunfish with a mealy worm and it was a bluegill. Angelo helped Gabriel release the fish after Steve took a picture of him holding the fish. Alex the helper was fishing for bass and he hooked a big one!

The fight was on. As the bass jumped out of the water and Alex was reeling the fish in when all of the sudden the line went loose. Alex went from being happy and excited to sad and disappointed. Steve walked over to Alex and said "That was a big bass that got away".

Checking the fishing line Steve determined that Alex had not tied a good fishing knot and the line worked loose from the swivel. Steve helped Alex attach another swivel and they double checked the knot again to insure that would not happen again.

Everybody was catching sunfish some students already had caught three or more. Darien had changed his fishing spot. He was watching his bobber when Rina came over to help him.

The bobber started to jump on top the water. Rina told Darien to set the hook. "I finally have a sunfish," thought Darien as he started to reel it in.

It was a blue gill. Steve took a picture of Darien and his first sunfish catch. The fish was about seven inches long. Steve told the boy they could get as big as twelve inches long and weigh about two pounds. Darien asked Rina to fish with him because he figured she was good luck. And he must have been right because he caught four more bluegills that day. Everyone caught at least two sunfish and Brandon caught a fish called the black crappie. Brendan caught a kool looking fish called a yellow perch.

Steve had the class thank Angelo and Rina for helping them fish and he told them they were great fishing guys and we said good bye.

Darien could not wait to get back to the college and tell his parents about catching four bluegill sunfish. When the bus pulled in he saw his Mom and Dad waiting.

Steve gave all the students their pictures that he had taken during the week. He promised to send them pictures of the fish they had caught that day. Next he handed out the casting contest certificates. The certificates had their pictures on them casting and what place they came in they were kool! "Hope to see you next year in fishing class," they said.

Darien and his Dad and Mom walked over to Steve to thank him. He than thanked the boy for taking his class. "You ought to enter that drawing of a brook trout in an art contest, Darien," Steve said. "You read the fishing literature I gave you and you did a really good job of interpreting it. I sure hope you take the fourth grade fishing class next summer."

On the drive home Darien looked at his casting certificate and pictures of his golden rainbow trout, chain pickerel, bass, and our class picture with his new friends.

Darien had thought about Steve rescuing the baby duckling at Moyers Lake and me and my fellow students trying to catch the baby eel at Mueller's Country Store.

"You know Mom and Dad," he said, "this was the best time I ever had."

Places We Fish

1. Beltsville State Park
2. Delaware River, Riegelsville Area
3. Green Lane Park
4. Jacobsburg Park
5. Kaercher Creek Park
6. Kernsville Dam
7. Leaser Lake
8. Lehigh River
9. Mauch Chunk Lake Park
10. Memorial State Park
11. Merrill Creek Reservoir
12. Monocacy Creek
13. Moyers Lake
14. Nockamixon State Park
15. Ontelaunee Creek
16. Saucon Park
17. Secret Ponds One and Two
18. The Little Lehigh

Favorite Bait Shops

1. Cabela's
2. Country Roads by Lake Minsi
3. Mac's Hobby Shop
4. Mike's Bait & Sport Shop
5. Moyer's Lake
6. Mueller's Country Store
7. Wal-Mart's

The Fishing with Steve Photo Section

Steve has always loved taking pictures of people, especially people fishing and showing off their catch. He wishes he had photos of himself when he started to fish.

The following photos are a random selection of students, parents and grandparents who all shared the joys of fishing with Steve. Steve hopes that these pictures will encourage others to enjoy fishing together,

I hope you enjoy the following photographs.

Louis still holds the record for the biggest bass

Tyler and his Golden Rainbow Trout

Adam at Secret Pond Two

Adam 2005

Adam posing with a 55 lb Snapping Turtle

Thomas catches a bass

Jonathan catches a Chain Pickerel at Mauch Chunk Lake Park

Jonathan at Leaser Lake

Joey at Kerns Creek Lake

Nice Frog now let him go

Tyler

Nice bass caught at Moyers Lake

Aaron

Another bass Moyers Lake

Justin at Kaercher Creek Lake

Jack at Moyers Lake

Forks Township gang at Moyers Lake

Ryan at Moyers Lake

Andrew under the bridge at
Nockamixon State Park

Lake Minsi

Wyatt with Perch

Steve and Wyatt

Wyatt a little taller

Tyler nice fishing hat

Alex at Secret Pond One

Jacob at Lake Minsi

Alex with Catfish

Austen happy about taking 1st place in casting contest

**Horizons for Youth Fishing Program
Northampton Community College
Casting Competition 2006**

First Place: Austen D. Hartzell

Instructor: Steve Goosley

Austen at Lake Minsi

Zachary at Lake Minsi

Grant at Moyers Lake

Corey and Kelsey at Moyers Lake

Joe at Mauch Chunk Lake

Quinten at Moyers Lake

Quinten and Andrew

47

William

William

Dave and son Jacob fishing at Lake Minsi

Howard and daughter Emily show off days catch

Nathan and children fishing at Lehigh Parkway

Jaime and son Justin catch a bass

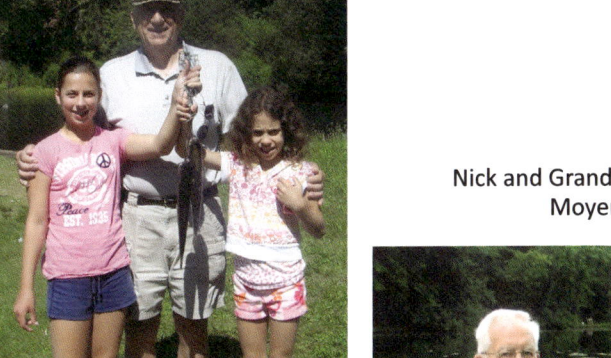

Nick and Grandfather fishing at Moyers Lake

Angelina and Brianna fishing with Grandfather

Joshua and Dad at Lake Minsi

Lutz and son Dylann who caught the bigger fish

Dad and Joey at Nockamixon State Park

Darien and his Uncle Steve at the Lehigh Parkway fishing contest

Ed my fishing assistant fishing with his grandchildren Bella and Chase

Derek fishing with Grandfather at Moyers Lake

Zachary fishing with Grandfather

Cabela's in Hamburg for bait and tackle before fishing Kerns Creek Lake

Gail from Moyers Lake shows students how to clean fish

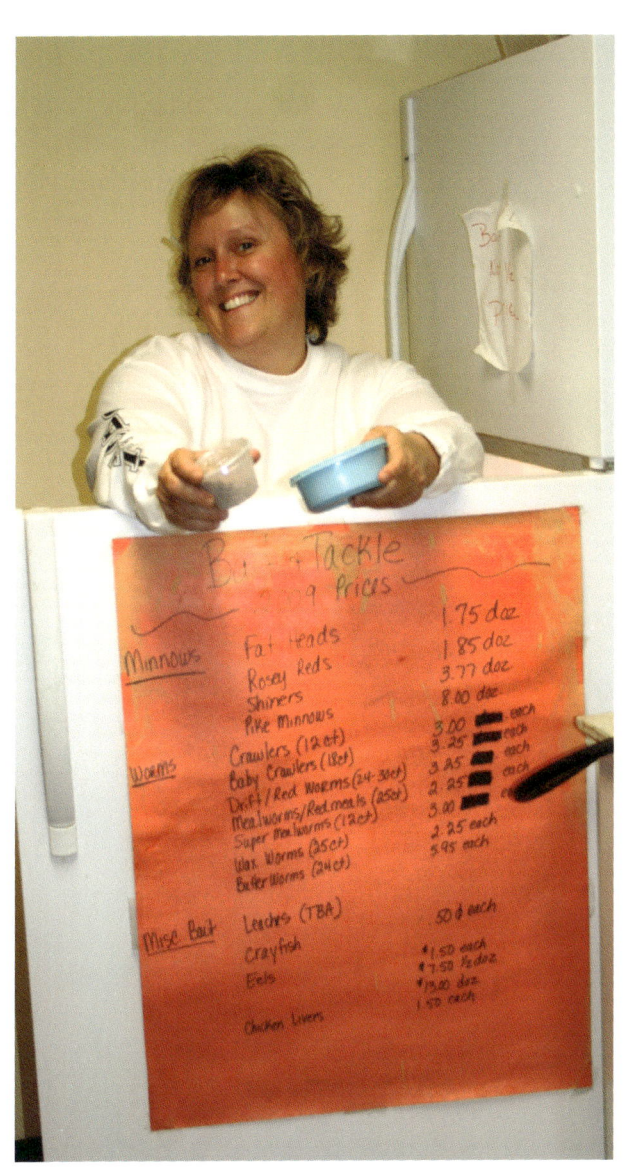

We stop at Mueller's for bait on the way to fish the Delaware River

Ray catches his first fish at Lease Lake with Steve

Robert and Daulton at Green Lane Park

Steve wearing his fishing glasses to protect his eyes from UV rays

Robert, Daulton, and Joey at Green Lane Park

Joey catches a Carp using the same secret bait

Zach at Green Lane Park

Sara catches Carp with our secret bait

Brianna fishing at Moyers Lake

Diana fishing at Moyers Lake

Gabriella fishing at Secret Pond Two

All Girls Class 2008 at Moyers Lake

Gabby is not afraid to handle live bait!

54

Jessica fishing at Moyers Lake

Rebecca nice Largemouth Bass

Lara helping out at Nockamixon State Park

Kyla nice sunfish

Maria at Moyers Lake

Catherine fishing at Lake Minsi

Donovan at Moyers Lake

Sierra with trout

Andrew with trout

Boating at Moyers Lake

Zachary and Rachel are having trout for diner

Row row row your boat if you can

Bob the bus driver catches a catfish

Zachary fishing from boat at Green Lane Park

Fish fry tonight

This poor duck got hooked

Hook removal was successful

Steve fishing at Lake Erie

Steve fishing at Lake Ferguson in Arizona

Sam and Steve catch a Sand Shark in Barnegat Bay, in New Jersey

Francesca and Martina

Francesca nice trout

Alimo from Italy at Lake Minsi

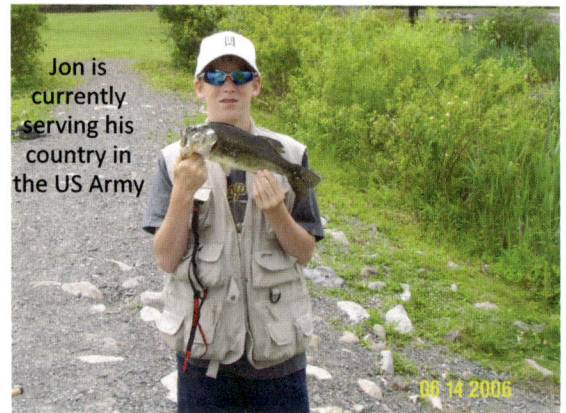

Jon is currently serving his country in the US Army

Martina catches a chain pickerel

Mike teaches students how to use fly rod

Jon caught this big Carp by his house

Alan shows the class his Angler Award from the Pennsylvania Fish Commission

Alan catches trout

Water snake at Lake Minsi

Justin at Moyers Lake

Claire catches a trout

Steve rescued Dodson the turtle and used him for show and tell and then released him in a safe area

Daniel fishing at Leaser Lake

Daniel and Nick having fun fishing

Brandon at Kerns Dam

Jeff at Nockamixon State Park

Nathan takes 1st place in casting contest

M'Kenna catches a bass

Nathan at Moyers Lake

Ashley catches a Large Mouth Bass at Secret Pond One

Daniel helps Steve with students one summer

Ashley helps the students catch fish

Anthony fishing at Mauch Chunk Lake

Alex, Joey, and Anthony rescue a baby bird

Nice catch Jacob

Mom, Jacob, and Andrew at Moyers trout pond

Jacob catches a trout

Steve and Naomi will always treasure the time they fished with Joe and Meryl at Barnegat Bay, in New Jersey